# FIN WHALES

## THE WHALE DISCOVERY LIBRARY

Sarah Palmer

Illustrated by Tony Gibbon

Rourke Enterprises, Inc.
Vero Beach, Florida 32964

**Library of Congress Cataloging-in-Publication Data**

Palmer, Sarah, 1955-
   Fin Whales.

   (The Whale discovery library)
   Includes index.
   Summary: Describes the physical characteristics,
habits, and natural environment of the world's
most common whale, the finback.
   1. Finback Whale—Juvenile literature.   [1. Finback
Whale.   2. Whales]   I. Title.   II. Series:
Palmer, Sarah, 1955-
Whale discovery library.
QL737.C424P344   1989        599.5'1        88-3274
ISBN 0-86592-479-1

Printed in the USA

# TABLE OF CONTENTS

| | |
|---|---|
| Fin Whales | 5 |
| How They Look | 6 |
| Where They Live | 9 |
| What They Eat | 11 |
| Living In The Ocean | 14 |
| Baby Fin Whales | 16 |
| Fin Whales and People | 19 |
| Saving Fin Whales | 20 |
| Fact File | 22 |
| Glossary | 23 |
| Index | 24 |

# FIN WHALES

The fin whale is the world's most common whale. It is also known as the "common rorqual." Fin whales are **baleen whales**. They have no teeth, and they trap food in their mouth using **baleen plates**. Fin whales can swim very fast. A close relative of the fin whale is the **Sei whale**. Sei whales look like fin whales but are smaller.

*Sei whales are like small fin whales*

# HOW THEY LOOK

Fin whales have a dark gray or brownish back and a pure white underside. They are medium-sized whales. Fin whales can grow up to 80 feet long and normally weigh about 65 tons. Very long **grooves** run right down their underside. These grooves are actually folds in the fin whales' skin. When the whales take in food and water, the folds stretch out so they can hold more in their mouth and throat.

*Fin whales have long grooves right down their undersides*

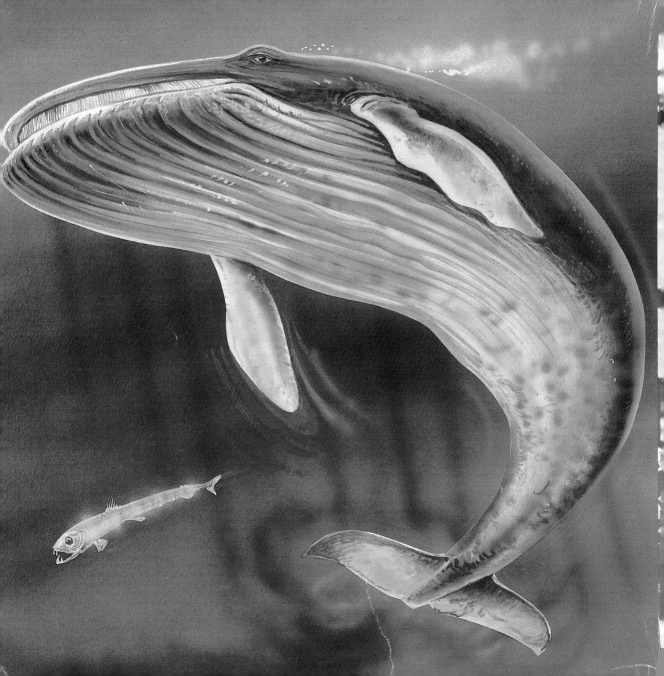

## WHERE THEY LIVE

Like other types of whales, fin whales are separated into two groups. One group lives in the north. Fin whales have been seen off Alaska and Canada, and even as far north as Greenland. The other group of fin whales lives in the southern oceans toward the South Pole. Most of the time fin whales like to live in deep water. Sometimes they come close to land.

*Fin whales like to live in deep, cold water*

# WHAT THEY EAT

**Herring**, a kind of fish, is the fin whales' favorite food. Fin whales have been watched hunting herrings. They swim around the herrings to push them together into a tight group. The fish see only the fin whale's pure white underside flashing past them. They are stunned by the quick movement and bright light. When the whale has herded the herrings close together, he opens up his great mouth and swallows them.

*Herring are the fin whales' favorite food*

*Fin whales can swim very fast*

Fin whales dive deep into the
ocean

# LIVING IN THE OCEAN

Fin whales like to live in deep water. Sometimes they dive deep into the water. They can stay underwater for up to an hour. Usually they stay under much less time than that. The whales come back to the surface of the water to breathe air. Sometimes they **spout** when they come back up. A fin whale's spout is more than 15 feet high.

*A fin whale's spout can be over 15 feet high*

## BABY FIN WHALES

The fin whale parents have a baby, or **calf**, every two years. Like most other whales, the fin whale calves are born during the winter when the family is in warmer waters closer to the **equator**. The fin whale calf is 22 feet long at birth. It can weigh as much as 4½ tons. Young fin whales stay close to their mothers for the first twelve months of their lives.

*Baby fin whales are born in warm water*

# FIN WHALES AND PEOPLE

Fin whales have been one of the most hunted whales. When blue whales became rare, the **whalers** started to hunt fin whales. The whalers called the fin whales "razorbacks" because they have a long ridge down their back. The whalers could catch several fin whales at once, because the whales all stayed together to help each other.

*Fin whales have a long ridge down their back*

## SAVING FIN WHALES

Fin whales have thick **blubber** to protect them from the cold. The blubber from one fin whale can make up to 8 tons of oil. Earlier in this century the whalers were killing 10,000 fin whales each year. They used the blubber for oil and the baleen plates or whale bone for corsets. Today fin whales are protected by law. Whalers can no longer kill them.

A large fin whale could upset a
small ship

# FACT FILE

| | |
|---|---|
| Common Name: | Fin Whale, Common Rorqual |
| Scientific Name: | Balaenoptera physalus |
| Type: | Baleen whale |
| Color: | Dark gray or brown |
| Size: | up to 80 feet |
| Weight: | average 65 tons |
| Number in World: | 120,000 |

## Glossary

**baleen whales** (BAL een WHALES) — whales that have baleen plates instead of teeth

**baleen plates** (BAL een PLATES) — whale bones used to strain food in a whale's mouth

**blubber** (BLUB ber) — a thick layer of fat under a whale's skin

**calf** (CALF) — a baby whale

**equator** (equ AT or) — imaginary line from east to west around the middle of the earth

**grooves** (GROOVES) — ridges

**herring** (HER ring) — a kind of fish

**sei whale** (SEI WHALE) — a kind of whale that looks like a small fin whale

**to spout** (SPOUT) — to breathe out a mixture of air and water high into the air

**whalers** (WHAL ers) — people who hunt whales

# INDEX

| | |
|---|---|
| baleen | 5, 20 |
| blubber | 20 |
| color | 22 |
| common rorqual | 5 |
| razorbacks | 19 |
| Sei whale | 5 |
| size | 22 |
| spout | 14 |
| weight | 22 |
| whalers | 19, 20 |